W9-CGX-848

Mirror Image
HOW GUYS SEE THEMSELVES

by Adam Woog

Content Adviser:
Billy AraJeJe Woods, Ph.D.,
Department of Psychology, Saddleback College,
Mission Viejo, California

Reading Adviser:
Alexa L. Sandmann, Ed.D.,
Professor of Literacy, College and Graduate School
of Education, Health and Human Services,
Kent State University

MONTCLAIR HIGH SCHOOL LIBRARY
MONTCLAIR, NEW JERSEY

Compass Point Books
151 Good Counsel Drive
P.O. Box 669
Mankato, MN 56002-0669

Copyright © 2009 by Compass Point Books
All rights reserved. No part of this book may be reproduced without written
permission from the publisher. The publisher takes no responsibility for the use of
any of the materials or methods described in this book, nor for the products thereof.
Printed in the United States of America.

This book was manufactured with paper containing
at least 10 percent post-consumer waste.

Photographs ©: Capstone Press/Karon Dubke, cover; PhotoEdit Inc./Michael Newman,
5, 17, 24, Tony Freeman, 14, Spencer Grant, 39, Don Smetzer, 41; Newscom, 7, 32, 42;
Shutterstock/Ian MacLellan, 8, Yuri Arcurs, 23, Talya, 27; Getty Images Inc./Time &
Life Pictures/Forrest Anderson, 9, Riser/Rob Van Petten, 20, UpperCut Images/Keith
Brofsky, 37; fotolia/Graca Victoria, 11; Landov LLC/UPI/Jim Ruymen, 13; Alamy/
PhotoStockFile/Tristan Hawke, 15, ACE STOCK LIMITED, 19, Leila Cutler, 29,
Bubbles Photolibrary/Angela Hampton, 30, Picture Partners, 34.

For Compass Point Books
Brenda Haugen, Bobbie Nuytten, Jo Miller, LuAnn Ascheman-Adams,
Joe Ewest, Nick Healy, and Catherine Neitge

For Bow Publications
Bonnie Szumski, Kim Turner, and Katy Harlowe

Ackowledgment: The author thanks Leslie R. Walker, M.D., adolescent
medicine specialist, Seattle Children's Hospital, for her generous gift of time
and expertise.

Library of Congress Cataloging-in-Publication Data
Woog, Adam
  Mirror image : how guys see themselves / by Adam Woog.
     p. cm.—(What's the Issue?)
  Includes index.
  ISBN 978-0-7565-4136-1 (library binding)
  1. Teenage boys—Psychology—Juvenile literature.
  2. Body image in adolescence—Juvenile literature.
  3. Self-perception in adolescence—Juvenile literature. 4. Mass media
and teenagers—Juvenile literature. I. Title. II. Series.
  HQ797.H55 2009
  155.5'32—dc22   2008045469

Visit Compass Point Books on the Internet at *www.compasspointbooks.com*
or e-mail your request to *custserv@compasspointbooks.com*

TABLE OF CONTENTS

CHAPTER one

WHY DO I LOOK LIKE THIS?

When Sam* has looked at himself in the mirror lately, he hasn't been satisfied. He thinks he needs more muscle. He wishes he didn't have to wear glasses. He'd like to have a stronger image of himself, both for himself and for his friends—stronger physically, stronger mentally. He wonders a lot about what he can do to change his image.

How about you? What do you see in the mirror? Is it just what you want? No, probably not exactly.

What do you think people see when they look at you? Is it just what you want? No, probably not exactly.

What you think about your body is your body image. It's part of your self-image, and it's not just about physical looks. How you feel about your body is part of how you feel about yourself as a person.

* This and other names in this book have been changed for privacy reasons.

Every guy has a certain way of thinking about his body. Sometimes it's different from reality. Some muscular guys, for instance, don't think of themselves as strong.

Experts generally agree that adolescent boys and girls have different body image issues. Maybe that's because in our society a lot of people expect boys to be coordinated and good at sports. Boys are also expected to be tough and able to stand up to pressure. Girls, on the other hand, are often expected to conform in other ways—for example, not to look or act tough or "boyish."

Some guys work hard to stay in great shape. Danny says, "I would like to be skinny, have a muscular figure to help with sports, and look good for myself." He works out and is

It's easy to focus on things you don't like about your body, but don't forget what's good.

fit. Still, he says, "Teens want to look like celebrities and rock stars. They want to follow the trends."

How you feel about your body has a huge impact on your life. Especially when you're an

Everybody's Different

Your rate of growth during your teen years and how much weight you put on can vary greatly. Typically, growth increases between 12 and 16 years old. You might put on 15 to 65 pounds (7 to 28 kilograms) and grow 4 to 12 inches (10 to 30 centimeters).

adolescent or a teen, body image is part of everything you do. It's part of deciding what kinds of clothes to wear. Whether you'll blend in or stand out. It can even affect your grades in school and how well you get along with friends and adults.

Your body image is tied up with your emotions. If you let it, body image can affect you for years to come. A poor body image can make you feel bad and inferior to others, but a healthy one can make you feel great.

What's Your Body Image?

There's probably no single definition of a good body image. It's going to be different for everyone. But there are some things that most guys would list.

Here are a few questions that might help you define your own body image:

- Do you feel coordinated most of the time?
- When you see yourself in a mirror, what do you notice first?
- How do you think of yourself when you imagine your body in your mind?
- What are you good at? Sports? Video games? Car repair? Does doing that thing well make you feel confident?
- Do you worry about your size and strength compared to other guys?
- How important are the right clothes and haircut to you?
- Do you worry about food

and your weight? Or do you eat what you want, when you want?

- If you could, what would you change about your body?

You probably already know what you don't like about your body. But by answering these questions, you've had a chance to remind yourself about what's good about being you. If you still can't find something positive about your body image, we'll need to dig deeper.

Family Matters

Your body image can affect your relationship with your family—especially if you don't look or act like them.

Sometimes not looking like your parents supports a good

Everybody has special talents. What are yours? Are you a whiz at working on engines, scoring goals in hockey, or playing video games?

body image. Ben says, "I have a good relationship with my parents, even though I'm adopted and don't look like them. They're both white and short, but I'm biracial—black and white. They're not athletic, but I'm on the soccer and basket-ball teams. And I'm, like, five or six inches taller than them!"

On the other hand, not looking and acting like your family can sometimes be a problem. Zack says, "I was always overweight when I was in middle school and high school. My mom and dad were really into staying thin and eating healthy. My mom was a fitness instructor and my dad played racquetball. I exercised, but not enough to keep my weight down. I really paid the price because kids teased me a lot."

Joining a sports team is a great way to make friends while helping to keep your body healthy.

Your Genes Fit You

For better or worse, your biological family has a lot to do with how you look. Body shape, eye and hair color, and skin tone are determined before you're even born. Blame your genes—the biological building blocks that control what you inherit from your parents.

You can't control genes. If

If your parents have weight issues, you'll probably inherit those same issues.

Genes, Genes, and More Genes!

Some of the characteristics you inherit from your parents come from a single gene. Others come from combinations of genes. Every person has from 25,000 to 35,000 genes. That makes an almost endless number of possible combinations that go into forming you.

your dad and mom are both tall, chances are you'll be tall. If they're short and stocky, you'll likely be the same way. If they have different body types from each other—well, you'll probably be a blend.

On the other hand, don't just give up because of your genetics. Where you live, how your parents raise you, what activities you do, how you eat and exercise—they also determine how your body develops. When people talk about "nature or nurture," this is what they mean. Also, proper diet and exercise might help you bulk up or slim down. Still, genetics will determine a lot about your ability to lose or gain weight and stay that way. So go ahead—blame your parents!

What's Happening With My Body?!

When you were a little kid, you probably didn't think a lot about your body. Kids are happy just to run around and play—*hey, look how high I can jump!*

But that changes, usually with adolescence, which can start as early as 9 or 10 or as late as 14 or 15. Around this time, boys start noticing how they differ from other kids and begin forming opinions about their own bodies.

This is usually a tough time. Kids wonder if their bodies are OK. They compare themselves to others. They decide which parts of their bodies they like— and which ones they hate.

Then, look out! Here comes puberty, the physical and mental changes happening as your body matures. Your hormones change, and so does your body. Your voice will deepen. You'll have growth spurts, stinky sweat, and armpit and genital hair.

The Path of Puberty

Typically, puberty starts between 9½ to 14 years of age. The first change is that your testicles get bigger. Penis enlargement begins approximately one year later. Pubic hair appears at about 13½ years of age. Other changes include hair under the arms and on the face, voice change, and acne, usually around 15 years of age. On average, boys take from two to a little more than four years to finish puberty, but everybody changes at a different pace.

A regular skin-care routine may help with a stubborn acne problem.

You might get acne.

Hormones don't just affect your body. They affect your mood, too. Almost everybody has mood swings during puberty that can suddenly turn a person from cheerful to depressed and back again.

Most people think that mood swings in puberty happen just with girls. But guys have mood swings, too, although they typically don't recognize it. Samantha says, "Teenage girls always

> "Teenage girls always know that boys have mood swings. The boys are like, 'No, no, we don't really have a problem,' and the girls are like, 'Oh, yeah they do!'"

know that boys have mood swings. The boys are like, 'No, no, we don't really have a problem,' and the girls are like, 'Oh, yeah they do!'"

11

CHAPTER two

DEVELOPING A REALISTIC BODY IMAGE

Pretend you can magically change your body to whatever you want. What would you change? Would you be taller? Have bigger muscles? Whiter teeth?

Now ask yourself some questions. What would make your body perfect? Would other people agree? And where did this image of the perfect body come from?

The answer to the last question may surprise you.

That's because for years society has been telling you how *it* thinks you should look. Ever since you were little, you've seen guys in advertisements, TV shows, and movies. Some of them are classically handsome. Others are super-masculine, rugged, and good-looking or athletic.

So by the time puberty hits, you have already received a zillion messages: You should look like *this*, not *that*. It's cool to act *this* way, not *that* way.

Many people think Tiger Woods is a guy's guy—handsome and athletic.

Teasing

Guys typically don't have much leeway in defining their looks. If you're not a "guy's guy"— athletic or coordinated or outgoing—you run the risk of teasing, bullying, or even beatings. It's all too common. If you don't fit in, you can get labeled as a wuss or a sissy.

Take Bob and Chris. Bob is in college and has a normal build. But as a young teen he was late in developing:

"I know everybody's different. Some kids start getting mustaches in elementary school! Their voices change and everything. I didn't."

"I know everybody's different. Some kids start getting mustaches in elementary school! Their voices change and everything. I didn't. I was short, like a

13

Teen Bullying

According to a national survey, about 25 percent of U.S. students in grades six through 10 are the targets of school bullies. Other findings:

- **One out of five kids admits to being a bully at least sometimes.**
- **Eight percent of students miss one day of class per month because of fear of bullies.**

little boy, and my voice was high. Guys made fun of me, especially in gym class— called me a girl, whatever. I wanted to die, and it got so bad that I asked my doctor for a note excusing me from gym. My dad told me he'd been the same way, so I guess it was my genes. I still feel bad about it."

Chris doesn't like his body either. He says, "I am tall and thin like my dad. I don't like it. I want to be bulkier, more muscular—

During adolescence, guys' bodies mature and grow at various rates.

like some of my friends. Look at my arms! I have no muscle!"

Being Competent

When you think about body image, you think about how you feel about your physical body. But connected to this basic idea of how you look are a lot of other issues that really have to do with emotions. For example, one issue is how competent you think you

Having a talent for creating music can help boost your confidence.

are at doing stuff.

Whatever that is can vary. It might be sports, but it could be playing video games, hunting, repairing cars, playing music, acting, or debating.

Being competent at an activity or sport might not seem connected to your body image. But there is a direct connection between feelings of competency and how you feel about your body. Sometimes it's negative. For instance, some experts worry that guys who spend a lot of time with games and game magazines get too concerned with looking muscular, because so many game characters are big and toned.

But it also can be positive. If you're good at something, it makes you feel good about yourself. Gaming is just one example—it gives you great hand-eye coordination. Being competent in an activity, maybe even being better than anybody else you know, boosts your confidence.

That's an important factor in building a positive body image.

Points to Remember

Here are some questions to ask yourself. They might help you remember that having a good body image is tied closely to how you feel about yourself as a person:

- Do you make negative comments to yourself about your body and your self-image? Try to think of something positive instead.
- Do your friends care about your appearance? If they make negative comments instead of supporting you, maybe it's time to find some new friends.
- What's your attitude about other guys who like to do stuff such as dancing, dressing colorfully, or sewing?
- Can you appreciate the ways in which your body is great? For example, does your ability

with video games mean that your hand-eye coordination is really good? Look for what's good about you. If you're honest with yourself, I'll bet you can find lots of things that make you great.

People are complex. The captain of the football team also might be great at sewing.

CHAPTER three

FITTING IN—AND STAYING FIT

Your peers—your friends, classmates, and others your age—can have a lot to do with how your body image develops. Peer pressure can be brutal. For most people, fitting in with others is important—and that's especially so when you're an adolescent.

A lot of peer pressure concerns body image.

You might not want to admit it, but the peer pressure is there. Shawn says, "No kid I know would admit there's peer pressure. They might say, 'Nobody's pressuring me. It's my own decision.' Or they'd say, 'Well, everybody around me was doing it, so I thought I'd try.' Nobody wants to admit that peer pressure exists, but it's there."

Balance

Maybe you tell yourself you don't care what other kids think. Maybe you really *don't* care. But if you're a fairly average kid, you do care—at least sometimes. Sometimes you worry a lot, because you want to fit in.

Worrying about fitting in is a normal part of development. Most adolescents want to do just that. All through your teens, you'll spend a lot of time and energy trying to figure out who you are, how to act, and how to look.

Do you and your friends dress alike? That's a sign of peer pressure.

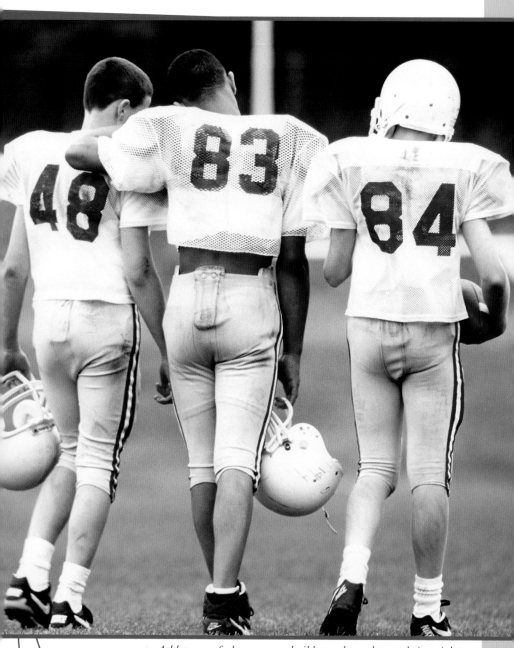

Athletes can feel pressure to build muscle or change their weight based on the sports they play.

Sometimes guys will try almost anything to find the right look and way to behave. And that can get out of hand. It's important to fit in, no doubt. It's also important to avoid going overboard. The trick is to find a balance. Remember: Bodies come in all shapes and sizes, and so do personalities. There's no one perfect look or way to act.

make a certain weight class for wrestling. Maybe you need to slim down for cross-country or bulk up for football.

No matter what your body type or what sport you play— or if you don't play any sport at all—you'll feel better if you're in shape. If you don't look and act the way other teens expect you to, you might be teased, bullied,

Making the Team

If you play a sport, the peer pressure is double. If you're athletic, you might fit in already with other athletic kids. But you have to be in shape, for instance, to play any sport well. And if you're on a team, getting along with your team-mates is important to playing a game well. That's also true, of course, for whatever you're into. It doesn't have to be just sports.

Getting in shape can mean a variety of things. Maybe you need to lose or gain pounds to

"I liked to read. I also liked unusual things for my age, like music and films from the 1940s. I just wanted to be left alone. But the jocks and other boys would tease me, call me fat."

or left out. What happens on the playing field or in the locker room can be cruel.

Zack recalls, "I liked to read. I also liked unusual things for my age, like music and films from the 1940s. I just wanted to be left alone. But the jocks and other boys would tease me, call me fat. Since I was never good at any of the sports, I dreaded P.E. In my senior year in high school I grew

What to Do When You're Bullied

Here are some tips on handling bullying:

- **Walk away if you can.**
- **Sit near the driver on the school bus.**
- **Take different routes to and from school. Get a friend or two to join you.**
- **Don't bring money or expensive things to school.**
- **Stay where other students and teachers are around.**
- **Avoid being in bathrooms or locker rooms by yourself.**
- **Talk to your parents, teachers, or counselors about it.**
- **Read your school's policy about bullying and talk with the principal about it.**
- **If there is no policy, investigate creating one.**

like six inches and I lost weight. Suddenly, people were more friendly. It kind of made me mad. I mean, where were these kids when I was fat?"

Look at Me!

Of course, not all guys try to fit in with a sports team—or any other organized group, for that matter. In fact, some guys reject fitting in. Maybe they go for a special look by getting an unusual haircut, or body art such as a piercing or tattoo.

But does dressing differently or getting body art really make you unique? It's hard to create that one-of-a-kind look. Most of the time, it's essentially like

If someone bullies you for any reason, tell a trusted adult.
No one deserves to live in fear.

someone else's. Goths and skaters are both groups with distinctive looks. But Goths look like other Goths, and skaters like other skaters.

A lot of times, trying to make a statement with the way you look is just a way to fit in with

The skateboarding culture has a look and style of its own.

a particular group, even if that group is out of the mainstream. Often you're just conforming to your group. There's nothing wrong with that. Sometimes it can even be a good thing.

Damon says, "I am very competitive in sports. However, I do feel some pressure to stay in shape by working out in the gym, for example. I love all kinds of sports—football, baseball, track, and golf to name a few. Let's face it, a teen who's tall and athletically built has an advantage on the field, so I do worry that I may stop growing, or become out of shape, which would affect my ability to compete."

Reach a healthy weight because it makes you feel good, not because you're afraid people are laughing at you or will bully you. Work out because it'll make you healthier, not just because your friends are. Dress a certain way because you like it, not because it's in fashion.

Those are sensible reasons to reach sensible goals. But sometimes being sensible doesn't have much to do with what guys do to change their body image.

"Let's face it, a teen who's tall and athletically built has an advantage on the field, so I do worry that I may stop growing, or become out of shape, which would affect my ability to compete."

CHAPTER four

I MIGHT HAVE A PROBLEM HERE ...

You may never be able to achieve the body image you want. You might never be really tall, or very well coordinated, or super slim. That doesn't stop some guys from trying to change their bodies to fit an ideal—and trying too hard can create problems.

Sometimes those problems are physical, sometimes they are mental, and sometimes a combination of both. In any case, they can be serious.

Biceps in a Bottle

For instance, there's been a boom lately in dietary supplements, such as protein powders and shakes that are taken with food. They promise to help you add weight and muscle mass. They're easy to get, and they promise wonderful results.

The issue is that not enough research has been done to know if dietary supplements are safe. Some experts question whether they work at all. Most doctors recommend avoiding them.

More is known about drugs called anabolic steroids, and what's known isn't good.

Steroids work for most people—they build amazing muscles quickly. But long-term steroid use can also cause big problems. Just consider these side-effects: reduced sperm count, shrinking testicles, impotence (the inability to have sex), difficulty urinating, hair loss, and male breast

Because little research has been done on the effectiveness of dietary supplements, doctors aren't sure how they affect an adolescent's growing body.

Dietary Supplements: Popular and Widespread

A 2005 study indicated that almost 5 percent of teen boys reported using some sort of dietary supplement at least weekly. Their use appears to be much higher among jocks: Another recent study indicated that 78 percent of high school athletes use dietary supplements regularly.

growth—not to mention the dangerous mood swings called 'roid rage.

Even scarier are the long-term, often permanent effects. Steroids can cause liver and kidney damage, as well as increased risk of stroke and heart attack. They also can trigger psychosis, a mental state characterized by bizarre behavior, hallucinations, and confused thinking. Anyone using anabolic steroids can expect a shortened life and serious health issues. One group of researchers estimates that

long-term use could take 10 to 20 years off your life.

All major professional athletic organizations ban steroids. Nonetheless, as sports fans know, they're widespread. Steroid scandals, such as recent ones in baseball and cycling, are all too common.

Not only are they dangerous and often illegal, supplements and steroids just don't work for adolescents. For most guys, it's just not physically possible to bulk way up until they're about age 15 to 17. You can get stronger, but you just aren't going to see the muscles before then. So the average middle-schooler isn't going to get a big benefit from steroids or supplements.

Anorexia, Bulimia, Binge Eating, and Bigorexia

There's another common problem related to the misuse of steroids and supplements—eating disorders. They happen when people have mental disorders that make them eat—or not eat—in extremely unhealthy ways. In the past, most people have thought that this is mostly a problem for girls. But lately it's become recognized as a serious problem for boys, too. It's estimated that one out of 10 boys has some kind of eating disorder. And studies indicate that the numbers of boys and men with eating disorders are rising sharply.

The best-known eating

disorder is anorexia. People with anorexia—about 25 percent of them boys and men—think they're overweight and horribly

About 28 percent of teenage boys are somewhat overweight.

fat when they're really not. Desperate to lose weight, they starve themselves. In extreme cases, they die if they don't get help.

Two other big problems are binge eating and bulimia. Binge eaters regularly overeat uncontrollably. An estimated 40 percent of binge eaters are male. People with bulimia go on eating binges and then force themselves to lose weight in unhealthy ways,

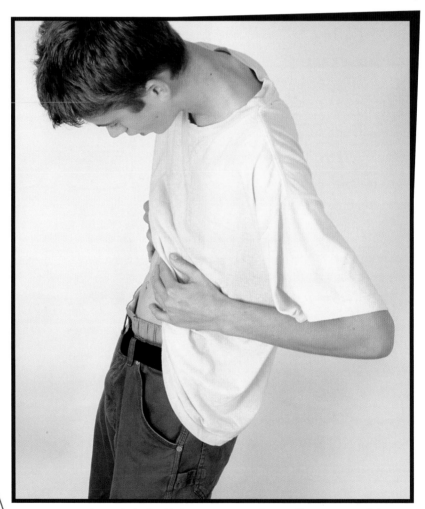

Anorexia is the third most common chronic illness among adolescents.

such as vomiting, using laxatives, or excessive exercise.

Less well known than these, but a big problem for guys, is sort of the opposite of anorexia. It's a condition called muscle dysmorphia, nicknamed "bigorexia." This happens when a healthy, muscular guy thinks that he's puny and frail.

Luke struggles with bigorexia. He says, "I'm a body-builder, no doubt about it. Maybe someday I can be a pro. I work out at least two hours a day, and I'm careful about what I eat. My friends, my parents, and my trainer all tell me that I'm in great shape. But it seems like no matter what I do I'm never satisfied. I always see flaws in my body, and I know I'm not strong enough. I guess I'll just have to keep working out more."

Too Much Exercise

A related problem is overexercis-ing. There's nothing wrong with moderate exercise. Everyone should get enough exercise to keep their bodies healthy. But it's possible to go too far, and studies show that exercising too much can do serious damage.

Bigorexia

It's estimated that about 10 percent of men who seriously work out have "bigorexia," ranging from mild to severe. Some experts think that this figure may actually be much higher.

"I'm in great shape. But it seems like no matter what I do I'm never satisfied. I always see flaws in my body, and I know I'm not strong enough."

This is especially true for teens, because it can damage their still-growing bodies. Experts say that overexercis-ing can lead to injuries such as bone fractures, muscle tears, and joint damage. In extreme cases, overexercising can permanently damage your growth plates, which are the weakest parts of your skeleton. This could keep you from reaching your full growth potential.

Lifting weights can help build muscles, but make sure to have an adult guide you with your workout plan. It's easy to harm your body if you don't know what you're doing.

Experts also caution that you should never exercise on your own, because the potential for injuring yourself is greater. Without guidance from a trainer, doctor, or coach, it's easy to exercise your muscles in the wrong ways.

There's yet another danger in exercising too much: getting addicted. Zack admits that he had an exercise addiction after he decided he could never go back to being fat. "I ran on the treadmill five miles every day, took my dog for extra long walks, and did 200 sit-ups on the floor of my room every day. I also tried really hard to eat as little as possible."

"I ran on the treadmill five miles every day, took my dog for extra long walks, and did 200 sit-ups on the floor of my room every day."

Helping a Friend

If you think a friend has a problem with an eating disorder, there are a number of things you can do to help.

- Ask questions. Don't blame or accuse, just try to get straight answers. Find out as much as you can. It can help to use "I" statements. For instance: "I'm

Under the Knife

Nearly 14,000 American boys ages 13 to 19 had surgery in 2006 to reduce the size of their breasts, according to the American Society of Plastic Surgeons. Many of the teens who had it done say that it significantly improved their body image.

Talking to a friend about his eating disorder might be a little scary, but you may be able to convince him to get the help he needs.

worried because you've been skipping lunch a lot," or "I'm a little nervous because it looks like you're getting obsessed with exercising." Repeat his answers back to make sure you have them right.

- Listen carefully. Try to understand—even if your friend is ashamed or scared and doesn't give you straight answers at first. Don't interrupt or be critical—this could make things worse.

- Tell your friend that you care. Show him that you want to help, because what he's doing is scary and unhealthy.

- Suggest an adult or a support group. Find someone you both trust that he can talk to. Offer to go along for support.

A Growing Industry

The diet industry is a $40 billion business. However, 95 percent of all dieters will regain their lost weight within one to five years. So the industry keeps growing!

If your friend refuses, consider whether you should go on your own and express your concerns about your friend. You might feel like you're betraying him, but you're not. You're doing your best to help him. He may need professional care.

CHAPTER five

HOW TO HAVE A HAPPY, HEALTHY, AND (MOSTLY) SANE BODY IMAGE

It's possible to have a healthy body—and a positive body image—without making yourself crazy. Really!

The key is to get comfortable with who you are. If you can accept what your body is (and isn't), you're on the right track. If you stay obsessed with being something that you're not, you'll torture yourself needlessly.

The first tip might be the hardest: Be patient. Bodies are tricky pieces of machinery, especially when you're an adolescent. The changes you're going through make your body awkward. For instance, after a growth spurt you'll probably be uncoordinated until you adjust. It's temporary. Be patient.

Another tip: Find someone to talk to. In our society, guys don't usually talk about stuff like body image with one another. In fact, they usually don't talk about their feelings very much at all. But find someone to talk to—a parent, a teacher, a member of the clergy, or some other trusted adult. Remember: They went through adolescence, too.

Oh Man, I'm So Fat/ Skinny/Whatever

Another tip is to stay sane about your weight, whether you want

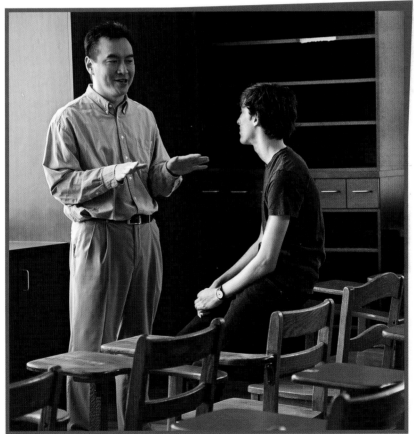

Don't be afraid to talk to a trusted adult about your feelings. He'll understand more than you think he will, and you will probably feel better.

to lose or gain. Don't rely too much on charts or formulas. They're useful guidelines, but guidelines can be misleading, because they're not tailored to individuals.

Consider this: Does your weight come from muscle or fat? If you work out a lot, you'll have more muscle, which weighs more than fat. You could be in great shape but still, by some guidelines, be overweight.

Guidelines can be misleading in other ways. For instance, you could be overweight but still score great on tests for important health factors such as heart disease, diabetes, and cholesterol. The bottom line: There isn't a magic formula that works for everybody.

Again, the key is to be realistic. You can't change your basic body type. That's genetics, remember? Genetics determines a lot about your natural weight. So instead of shooting for an unrealistic goal, work with what you have. Otherwise you're setting yourself up for failure.

Ask yourself: At what weight do I feel best? Do I feel strong and energetic? Can I lead a healthy, normal life? Have I got the energy to hang with my friends, play sports, and focus in school? If the answers are yes, then maybe you're at the right weight.

On the other hand, answer these questions: Do I get tired too easily? Am I often anxious or angry? If the answers are "yes," you're probably not at the right weight.

Obviously a big part of finding your best weight is to eat sensibly. It's mostly common sense: Avoid fad diets. Eat from all of the basic food groups. Eat at regular intervals—don't go too long without food. That way your blood sugar stays even, and you don't compensate by overeating. Watch out for fats,

Eating a balanced diet will help you maintain a healthy weight.

processed sugar, and salt. And don't eat too much. The calories you take in should equal the calories you burn off in exercise and daily living.

If you can do all that, your body will naturally find a balance.

Exercise

Along with eating goes exercise. Organized sports aren't for everyone, of course. You may not

A Million Guys With Eating Disorders

The National Eating Disorders Association estimates that more than 11 million Americans have an eating disorder. Only about one-tenth of those are male—but that's still about a million guys! And the numbers will probably go up.

want to play soccer or football. Still, you do owe it to yourself to get physical activity. Many experts recommend moderate exercise for at least 30 minutes several days a week. This is the bare minimum your body needs. An hour a day would be better!

Regular, moderate exercise isn't the same as a full workout. It might be something as simple as walking the dog, a pickup basketball game, or swimming laps.

As long as the exercise helps you feel fit and healthy, you've chosen well. That's the important part. Exercise even improves your mental outlook. That's

because hormonelike substances called endorphins are released when you exercise. They're natural painkillers and make you feel good—it's sometimes called the "runner's high."

And no, playing your Xbox doesn't count as exercise. Sorry.

It also doesn't count if you have a really great-looking avatar in an online game or a good-looking public image on MySpace. Online activity can be good in some ways. You can have friends all over the world. However, being online can't substitute for real exercise or face-to-face time with real friends.

A game of basketball with your neighborhood friends is great exercise.

Being Proud of Yourself

Maybe you don't have the body of your dreams. That's OK. You don't have to love every part of yourself, all the time, to be healthy and have a healthy body image.

You do, however, have to *accept* your body. Find out what makes you special. Quit imagining that everyone's looking at your flaws. They're not. They're much more worried about themselves. Start being nicer to yourself. Choose friends who like you the way you are. And find qualities in yourself that you like and that aren't related to your appearance. Don't let your looks define you.

Keep in mind that your physical body doesn't define your worth as a person. In our society, "masculinity" usually means being tough and showing little emotion. But being a well-rounded guy can also include having such qualities as sensitivity, patience, or being artistic. Being muscular and athletic isn't all there is to being a guy.

If you can do that, or at least a part of that, you might just discover that you like yourself—including your one-of-a-kind body. Whatever your shape, you can be proud of who you are.

Choosing friends who like the real you and the things you enjoy doing can make life a lot more fun.

QUIZ

Here's a quick quiz that can help you identify problems and strengths in your own body image.

1. Do you get moderate exercise three to five times a week?

2. Do you avoid diet supplements?

3. Is there someone (a friend or trusted adult) you can talk to if you have body image questions?

4. Do your parents and others around you watch out for their health?

5. Are there some things you're good at that are not related to appearance? For example, can you play a musical instrument or are you a whiz at computer games or at repairing engines?

6. Do you eat in a healthy way, avoiding overeating, undereating, or other dangerous habits?

7. Do you avoid habits such as smoking or drug or alcohol use?

How'd you do?

If you answered "Yes" 0-2 times: You may need to address some body image issues.

If you answered "Yes" 3-4 times: You could probably do better.

If you answered "Yes" 5-6 times: You're doing really well.

If you answered "Yes" 7 times: You're a champ!

GLOSSARY

adolescence | period of life between puberty and adulthood

anabolic steroids | synthetic hormones used to stimulate muscle size and strength

anorexia | eating disorder characterized by self-starvation and excessive weight loss

body image | set of thoughts, opinions, and feelings about one's looks and body shape

bulimia | eating disorder characterized by cycles of overeating and purging (by vomiting or diuretic/laxative intake)

eating disorders | mental disorders that center on eating too much or too little

genes | basic units of heredity; your genes determine your physical features such as height, skin color, hair color, and body shape

muscle dysmorphia | mental disorder, sometimes called bigorexia, in which people who are in good shape are convinced that they are not

puberty | period when a child's body develops adult features

'roid rage | nickname for the dangerous mood swings and aggression caused by the abuse of steroids

WHERE TO GET HELP

**Adolescent Crisis Intervention
& Counseling Nineline**
800/999-9999
*Young people can call this nationwide
hotline for help with problems such as
bullying, depression, abuse, drug addiction,
and more. The Nineline offers crisis counseling, referrals, and information services to
young people and their families.*

The Boys Projects
535 E. 12th St.
New York, NY 10009
212/505-3184
*This group's "no girls allowed" program
for elementary, middle, and high school
boys lets them examine issues such as media
messages, body image, and puberty in a
safe environment.*

Boys Town National Hotline
14100 Crawford St.
Boys Town, NE 68010
800/448-3000
*Anyone can call the Boys Town hotline
for help with any problem at any time.
Trained counselors are available to help
with questions and difficulties of all kinds.*

EDIN
124 Church St.
Decatur, GA 30030
404/816-3346
*This nonprofit group, based in a suburb of
Atlanta, Georgia, is dedicated to education
about eating disorders, such as anorexia
and compulsive overeating.*

**Harris Center for Education
and Advocacy in Eating Disorders**
2 Longfellow Place
Suite 200
Boston, MA 02114
617/726-8470
*The Harris Center, associated with Har-
vard University, conducts research and
education focusing on ways to promote
healthy development and eating habits for
children and adults.*

**National Association of Anorexia
Nervosa and Associated Disorders**
P.O. Box 7
Highland Park, IL 60035
847/831-3438
*Founded in 1976, this is the oldest eating-
disorders organization in America. It
provides free services in a number of areas
connected with eating disorders.*

National Eating Disorders Association
603 Stewart St.
Suite 803
Seattle, WA 98101
206/382-3587
hotline: 800/931-2237
*This nonprofit organization, a major
clearinghouse of information on eating
disorders, is dedicated to helping individuals and families affected by the problem.*

SOURCE NOTES

Chapter 1

Page 5, column 1, line 25: Danny. Chicago, Illinois. Personal interview. 2 Oct. 2008.

Page 8, column 1, line 1: Ben. Seattle, Washington. Personal interview. 24 Aug. 2008.

Page 8, column 2, line 6: Zack. Atlanta, Georgia. Personal interview. 2 Oct. 2008.

Page 11, column 2, line 3: Samantha. Seattle. Personal interview. 29 Aug. 2008.

Chapter 2

Page 13, column 2, line 4: Bob. Seattle. Personal interview. 13 Aug. 2008.

Page 14, column 1, line 13: Chris. San Diego, California. Personal interview. 2 Oct. 2008.

Chapter 3

Page 18, line 15: Shawn. Tacoma, Washington. Personal interview. 30 July 2008.

Page 21, column 2, line 15: Zack.

Page 25, column 1, line 7: Damon. San Diego. Personal interview. 3 Oct. 2008.

Chapter 4

Page 31, column 1, line 12: Luke. Seattle. Personal interview. 20 Aug. 2008.

Page 33, column 1, line 16: Zack.

ADDITIONAL RESOURCES

Fiction

Deuker, Carl. *Gym Candy*. New York: Houghton Mifflin Company, 2007.

Heiman, Herb. *Running on Dreams*. Shawnee Mission, Kan.: Autism Asperger Publishing Company, 2006.

McCormick, Patricia. *Cut*. New York: Push/Scholastic, 2002.

Stevenson, Robin. *Big Guy*. Custer, Wash.: Orca Book Publishers, 2008.

Nonfiction

Jeune, Veronique le. *Feeling Freakish? How to Be Comfortable in Your Own Skin*. Trans. Sophie Hawkes. New York: Amulet Books, 2004.

Kirberger, Kimberly. *No Body's Perfect: Stories by Teens About Body Image, Self-Acceptance, and the Search for Identity*. New York: Scholastic, 2003.

Wilhelm, Sabine. *Feeling Good About the Way You Look: A Program for Overcoming Body Image Problems*. New York: Guilford Press, 2006.

Willett, Edward. *Negative Body Image*. New York: Rosen Publishing, 2007.

For more information on this topic, use FactHound.

1. Go to *www.facthound.com*

2. Choose your grade level.

3. Begin your search.

This book's ID number is 9780756541361

FactHound will find the best sites for you.

INDEX

ABOUT THE AUTHOR

Adam Woog has written more than 60 books for adults, young adults, and children. He lives in Seattle, Washington, with his wife, who is a mental health therapist, and their teenage daughter.

ABOUT THE CONTENT ADVISER

Billy AraJeJe Woods has a doctorate in psychology, a master's in education, and a bachelor's in psychology. He has been counseling individuals and families for more than 25 years. He is a certified transactional analysis counselor and a drug and alcohol abuse counselor. A professor of psychology at Saddleback College, Mission Viejo, California, Woods teaches potential counselors to work with dysfunctional families and special populations. He began his counseling career in the military where he worked with men and women suffering from post-traumatic stress disorder. In his practice, Woods has worked with many young adults on issues related to drug and alcohol abuse and body image.